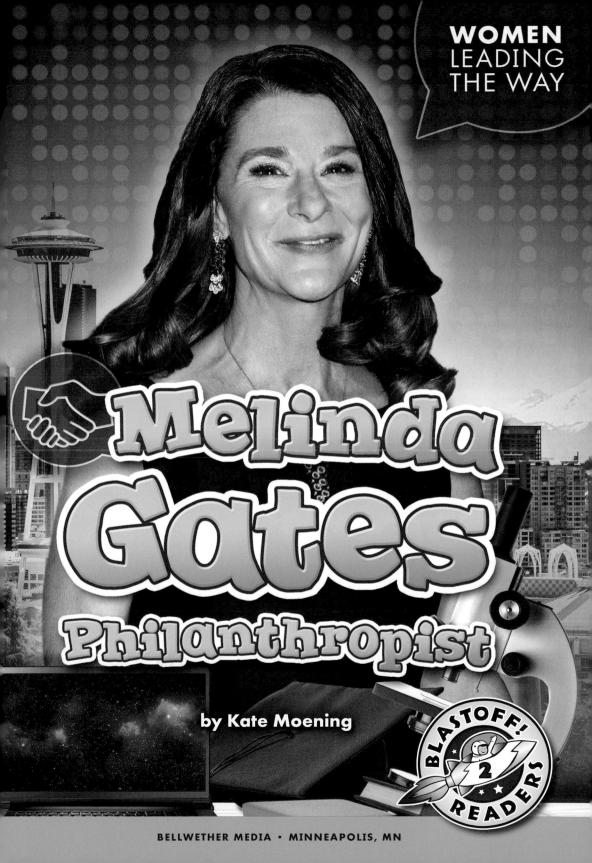

WOMEN LEADING THE WAY

Melinda Gates

Philanthropist

by Kate Moening

BLASTOFF! READERS
2

BELLWETHER MEDIA • MINNEAPOLIS, MN

Note to Librarians, Teachers, and Parents:

Blastoff! Readers are carefully developed by literacy experts and combine standards-based content with developmentally appropriate text.

Level 1 provides the most support through repetition of high-frequency words, light text, predictable sentence patterns, and strong visual support.

Level 2 offers early readers a bit more challenge through varied simple sentences, increased text load, and less repetition of high-frequency words.

Level 3 advances early-fluent readers toward fluency through increased text and concept load, less reliance on visuals, longer sentences, and more literary language.

Level 4 builds reading stamina by providing more text per page, increased use of punctuation, greater variation in sentence patterns, and increasingly challenging vocabulary.

Level 5 encourages children to move from "learning to read" to "reading to learn" by providing even more text, varied writing styles, and less familiar topics.

Whichever book is right for your reader, Blastoff! Readers are the perfect books to build confidence and encourage a love of reading that will last a lifetime!

This edition first published in 2020 by Bellwether Media, Inc.

No part of this publication may be reproduced in whole or in part without written permission of the publisher. For information regarding permission, write to Bellwether Media, Inc., Attention: Permissions Department, 6012 Blue Circle Drive, Minnetonka, MN 55343.

Library of Congress Cataloging-in-Publication Data

Names: Moening, Kate, author.
Title: Melinda Gates : Philanthropist / Kate Moening.
Description: Minneapolis : Bellwether Media, 2020. | Series: Women leading the way | Includes bibliographical references and index. | Audience: Ages 5-8 | Audience: Grades K-1 | Summary: ""Relevant images match informative text in this introduction to Melinda Gates. Intended for students in kindergarten through third grade"-Provided by publisher"–Provided by publisher.
Identifiers: LCCN 2019024614 (print) | LCCN 2019024615 (ebook) | ISBN 9781644871218 (library binding) | ISBN 9781618917973 (paperback) | ISBN 9781618917775 (ebook)
Subjects: LCSH: Gates, Melinda, 1964–Juvenile literature. | Philanthropists–United States–Juvenile literature.
Classification: LCC HV91 .M64 2020 (print) | LCC HV91 (ebook) | DDC 361.7/4092 [B]–dc23
LC record available at https://lccn.loc.gov/2019024614
LC ebook record available at https://lccn.loc.gov/2019024615

Editor: Al Albertson   Designer: Andrea Schneider

Printed in the United States of America, North Mankato, MN.

Table of Contents

Melinda Gates is a **philanthropist**. She and her husband, Bill, run the Bill and Melinda Gates **Foundation**.

It is one of the largest foundations in the world!

the Bill and Melinda Gates Foundation headquarters

4

"EVERYONE'S VOICE **DESERVES** TO BE HEARD." (2011)

Melinda grew up in Texas. She was the leader of her high school's dance team!

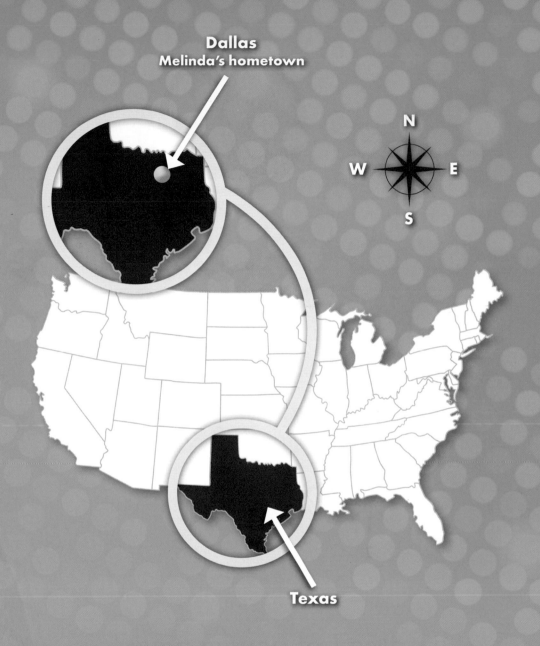

Dallas
Melinda's hometown

N
W E
S

Texas

Melinda's math teacher taught her to **program** computers.

Getting Her Start

Melinda and her husband, Bill

Melinda studied **computer science** in college. After that, she worked at the computer **company** Microsoft.

There, she met Bill. He was Microsoft's **CEO**.

Melinda Gates Profile

Birthday: August 15, 1964

Hometown: Dallas, Texas

Field: philanthropy, business

Schooling:
- studied computer science, economics, and business

Influences:
- Elaine and Raymond French (parents)
- Susan Bauer (high school math teacher)

Melinda and Bill were the world's richest people. But they saw that many people lived in **poverty**. Melinda wanted to help.

In 2000, Melinda and Bill started their foundation.

Melinda visiting a hospital in Africa

11

Changing the World

Melinda and Bill receiving the Medal of Freedom for their work

Melinda and Bill wanted to end poverty. They also wanted everyone to have **health care**.

Later, Melinda also wanted to help women and girls go to school.

Melinda talking to students

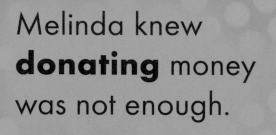

Melinda knew **donating** money was not enough.

In many countries, she helped **nonprofits** and governments work together. Melinda knew this could make her work last.

Melinda visiting the president of Uganda

Running the foundation was hard.
Sometimes people listened more
to Bill than Melinda.

But Melinda was strong.
She helped the foundation grow!

Melinda's Future

Today, Melinda still leads the foundation!

Melinda Gates Timeline

1987 Melinda starts working at Microsoft

2000 Melinda and Bill start the Bill and Melinda Gates Foundation

2004 *Forbes* magazine names Melinda one of the "100 Most Powerful Women" for the first time

2016 Melinda receives the Presidential Medal of Freedom from President Obama

2019 Melinda publishes her first book, *The Moment of Lift*, about empowering women

She helps people all over the world get **vaccines**. She helps women in poverty start businesses.

Melinda also hopes to **empower** other people to give back.

She knows communities become stronger when people work together!

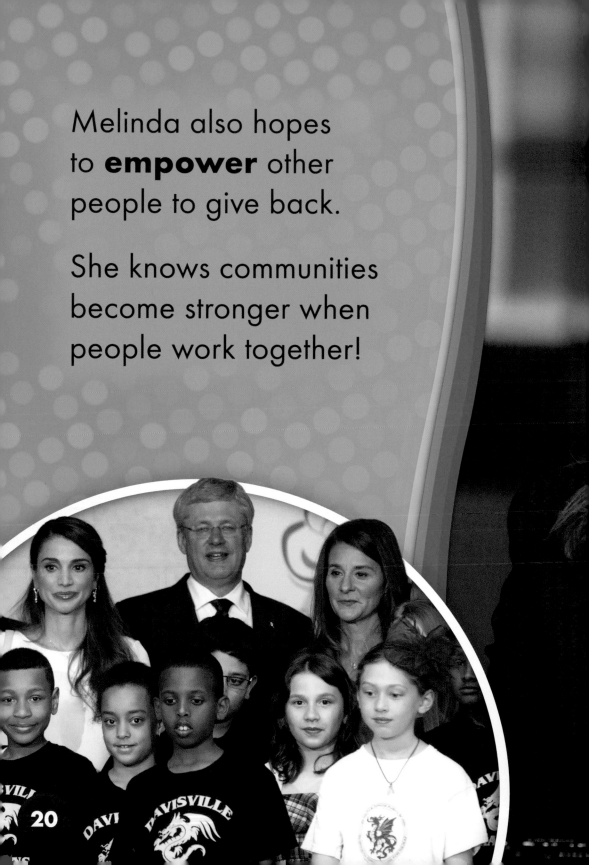

"**STAY TRUE**
TO WHAT YOU
BELIEVE IN."
(2012)

Glossary

CEO—the highest-ranking person in a company; CEO stands for "chief executive officer."

company—a group that makes, buys, or sells goods for money

computer science—the study of computers and their uses

donating—giving to help another person or group

empower—to give power, encouragement, or resources to someone

foundation—a group that gives money in order to do something that helps society

health care—treatment for illnesses from doctors

nonprofits—businesses that use all the money they earn to help people and run the business; nonprofits do not keep extra money for themselves.

philanthropist—a person who gives money and time to help make life better for other people

poverty—the state of not having enough money or resources to meet basic needs, such as food, clothing, or shelter

program—to give a computer a set of instructions to perform a specific task

vaccines—substances that are given to protect the body from specific illnesses

To Learn More

AT THE LIBRARY

Adams, Julia. *101 Awesome Women Who Changed Our World*. London, U.K.: Arcturus Publishing, 2018.

Lopez, Elizabeth Anderson. *Fantastic Kids: Helping Others*. Huntington Beach, Calif.: Teacher Created Materials, 2018.

Moening, Kate. *Malala Yousafzai: Education Activist*. Minneapolis, Minn.: Bellwether Media, 2019.

ON THE WEB

FACTSURFER

Factsurfer.com gives you a safe, fun way to find more information.

1. Go to www.factsurfer.com.

2. Enter "Melinda Gates" into the search box and click 🔍.

3. Select your book cover to see a list of related web sites.

Index